Tony the Shoemaker

DOMINIE FACTIVITY SERIES

Ellen Kronowitz

Dominie Press, Inc.

Publisher: Christine Yuen
Series Editors: Adria F. Klein & Alan Trussell-Cullen
Editor: Bob Rowland
Illustrator: David Preston Smith
Designers: Gary Hamada & Lois Stanfield

Published by:

Dominie Press, Inc.

1949 Kellogg Avenue
Carlsbad, California 92008 USA

www.dominie.com

ISBN 0-7685-0604-2

Printed in Singapore by PH Productions Pte Ltd

1 2 3 4 5 6 PH 02 01 00

Table of Contents

Welcome
Tony the
shoemaker

Jose Castro invited Tony the shoemaker to come to class at sharing time.

Tony the shoemaker told us about his life in Italy before he came to America.

"I was born in a little village," he said. "My father was the only shoemaker in the village."

“My father taught me how to make shoes. In those days, shoemakers made shoes by hand.”

7.5
152-DRESS PUMPS CARA

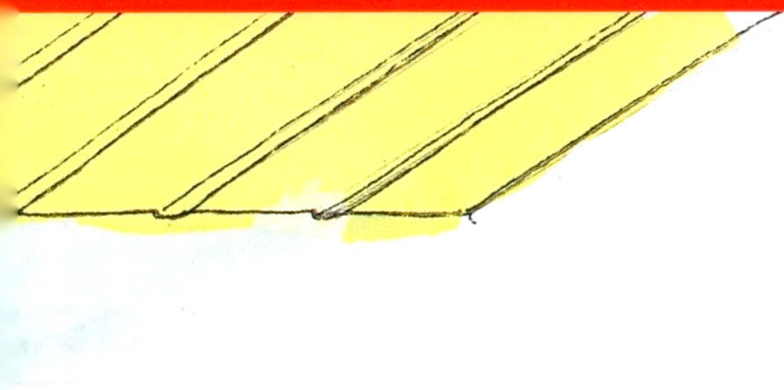

“Today, most shoes are made by machines in large factories.”

TONY'S
SHOE
REPAIR
GLUE

“Most shoemakers don’t make shoes by hand anymore. Instead, they fix shoes made by machines.”

Tony the shoemaker laughed. “We should call ourselves shoe fixers!” he said.

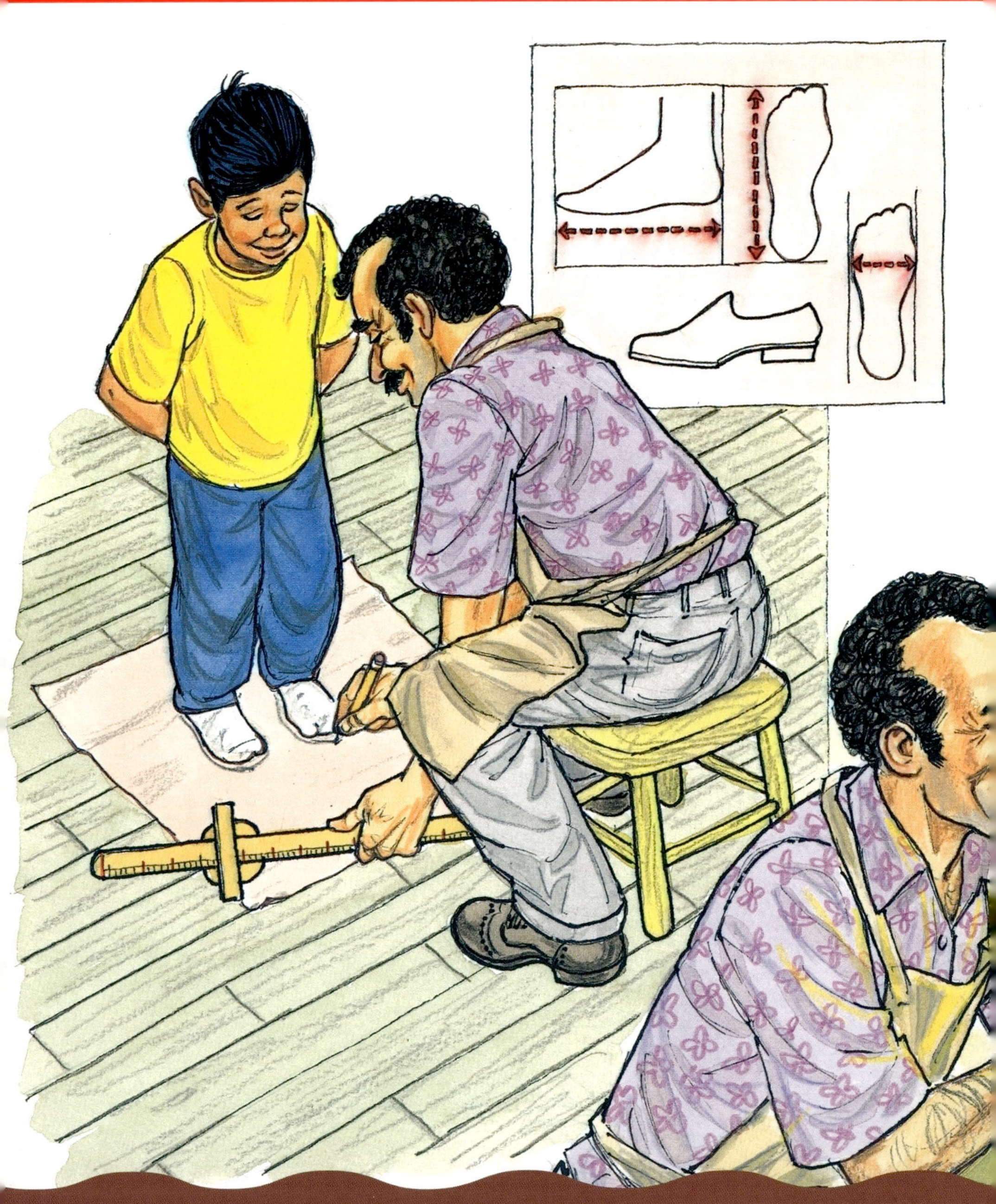

"But I still make shoes by hand. I am a shoemaker as well as a shoe fixer! This is how I made these shoes for Jose. First I measured his foot. Then I cut the leather for the tops and the soles."

TONY'S
SHOE
BLACK

"I sew the shoes together by machine, and I polish them by hand."

"I am proud of all the shoes I make," said Tony the shoemaker. "My customers are happy wearing them, too! Aren't they, Jose?"

"Yes!" said Jose, with a big grin.

Picture Glossary

factories:

machines:

leather:

shoemaker:

Index